SCHOLASTIC
LITERACY PLACE®

Hometowns

Copyright acknowledgments and credits appear on page 136, which constitutes an extension of this copyright page.

Copyright © 2000 by Scholastic Inc.   All rights reserved.   Printed in the U.S.A.

ISBN 0-439-06146-6

7 8 9 10   09   05 04 03 02

TABLE OF CONTENTS

Hometowns

THEME
We are all members
of a community.

UNIT 6

Hometowns

Hometowns

THEME
We are all members of a community.

UNIT 6

Welcome to

LITERACY PLACE

Come to a Mayor's Office

We are all members of a community.

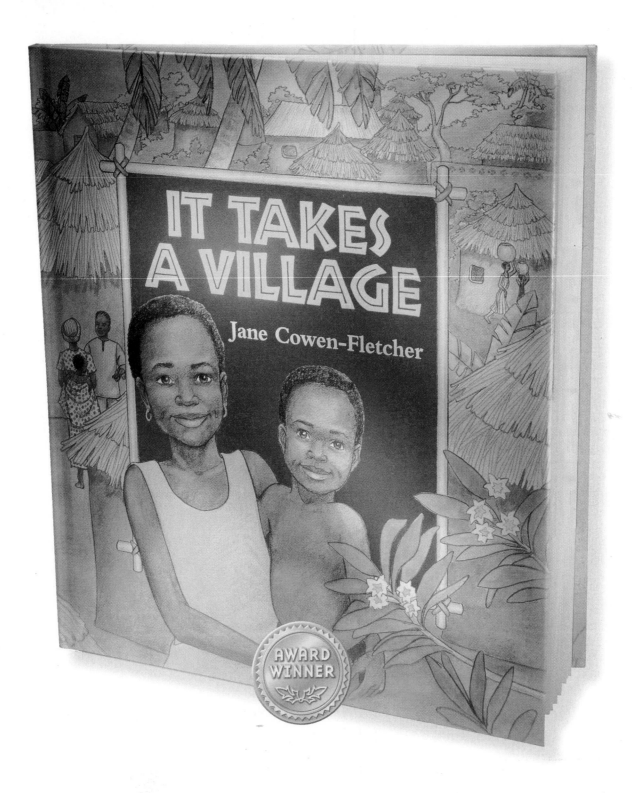

IT TAKES
A VILLAGE

Jane Cowen-Fletcher

AWARD
WINNER

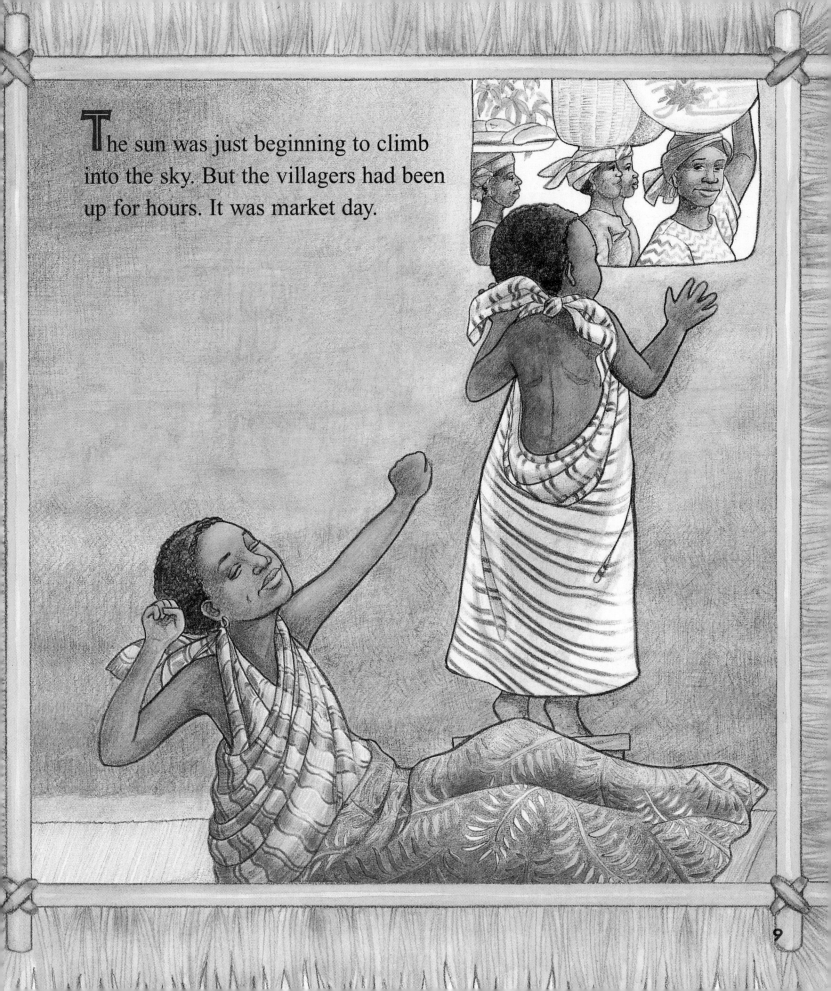

The sun was just beginning to climb into the sky. But the villagers had been up for hours. It was market day.

"Yemi," Mama said, "you must take care of your little brother today while we're at the market. I will be too busy selling our mangoes."

"Come, Kokou," Yemi said, "I will watch you today, all by myself!"

"All by yourself?" Mama asked, and smiled at what Yemi said. Mama knew better.

Mama picked up their mangoes. Yemi picked up Kokou. She felt very grown-up as she walked out of the family compound beside Mama.

11

They joined the stream of people walking into the village.
People came from all around to sell their goods and buy
whatever they needed. Market day was also a time for visiting.

The greetings started the moment
they stepped on the paths into town.
"Hello!"
"How are you?"
"How is your family?"

Yemi helped Mama set out their mangoes.
One of the other fruit vendors said, "Yemi is
a big girl now. She is a lot of help to you!"

"Yes," said Mama, "she is going to watch Kokou for me today."

"All by myself," Yemi added.

"All by yourself? *Yay gay!*" the women marveled. They smiled and nodded, but they knew better, too.

When the mangoes were all in neat piles, Yemi asked if she and Kokou could take a look around the market. Mama said, "Yes, but don't be gone too long."

Yemi had not walked very far when Kokou became restless. "He must be hungry," she said. She set him down for just one minute so she could buy some peanuts . . .

. . . and Kokou wandered off.

"*Cho*!" Yemi cried when she turned around and discovered Kokou was gone. She put the peanuts in her pocket . . .

. . . and she hurried off to find him.

"Where could he have gone?" she said.
As Yemi searched for him, she began to worry.
"Kokou must be hungry."

But he was not.

21

"Kokou must be thirsty."

But he was not.

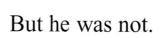

"Kokou must be frightened."

But he was not.

"Kokou must be hot."

But he was not.

"Kokou must be tired."

But he was not.

Finally, after searching for him everywhere,
Yemi stopped and cried aloud, "Kokou must be lost!"

But he was not.
Just across the path from
where Yemi stood, Kokou was
waking up.
"Is this your Kokou?" the
mat vendor asked.

27

"Yes!" exclaimed Yemi as she scooped up her brother.

"Thank you so much
for taking care of him,"
Yemi said to the mat vendor.

"Oh," he chuckled, "I
was not the only one." He
pointed to where Kokou
had come from.

Yemi thanked him again
and headed off in that
direction.

She said, "Thank you,"
again . . .

and again . . .

and again . . .

and again.

31

"We've been gone a long time, Kokou,"
Yemi said. "Mama must be worried."

But she was not. Mama knew better. "As my mama told me, and her mama told her, I will tell you. You weren't alone today, Yemi. We don't raise our children by ourselves. 'It takes a village to raise a child.'"

FROM

Gathering the Sun

An Alphabet in Spanish and English

Alma Flor Ada
English translation by Rosa Zubizarreta
Illustrations by **Simón Silva**

Kiosco de Cerezas

Cerezas en el kiosco
al lado del camino.
Redondas, rojas, lisas,
saludando al que pasa
como sonrisas.

Cherry Stand

Cherries for sale
at a roadside stand.
Round and red,
their smooth smiles
greet everyone who passes by.

CHERRIES

THINK ABOUT READING

Answer the questions on the story map. Write the answers on another piece of paper.

CHARACTERS

1. Who are the main characters in the story?

↓

PROBLEM

2. What does Mama ask Yemi to do?

3. What does Kokou do while Yemi buys peanuts?

↓

ENDING

4. Who takes care of Kokou?

5. What lesson does Yemi learn?

WRITE A THANK-YOU CARD

Yemi was glad so many people had helped her take care of Kokou. Make a thank-you card she could give to someone in the village. Draw a picture on the front of the card. Inside, write why Yemi is glad that so many people helped her.

LITERATURE CIRCLE

How do you think Yemi felt when she lost Kokou? What might she have been thinking? Imagine you are Yemi and tell about your day.

AUTHOR
JANE COWEN-FLETCHER

How does Jane Cowen-Fletcher know so much about an African village? She lived in Benin, a country in west Africa. There, Cowen-Fletcher got to know children like Yemi and Kokou. She also heard a popular saying: "It takes a village to raise a child." Knowing the children and the saying made Cowen-Fletcher want to write this book.

**ANOTHER BOOK BY
JANE COWEN-FLETCHER**

• <u>Mamma Zooms</u>

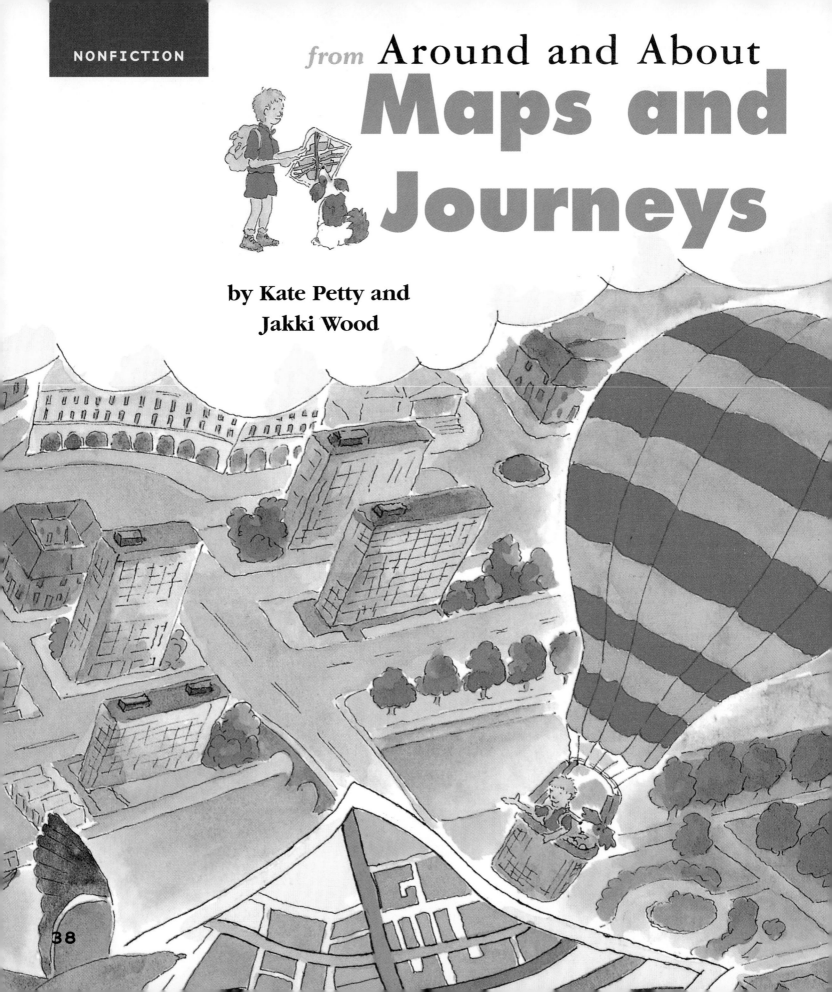

from Around and About

Maps and Journeys

by Kate Petty and
Jakki Wood

Don't get lost

Meet Harry and his dog, Ralph.
They like to travel all over the place.
Harry wants to find his way around
without getting lost, so he's going to
learn about maps.

A view from above

When Harry and Ralph walk along
the street, they can't see what's around the
corner. But when they look down from a
balloon, they can see everything laid out.
They can see the church and
the station and all the
roads in between.

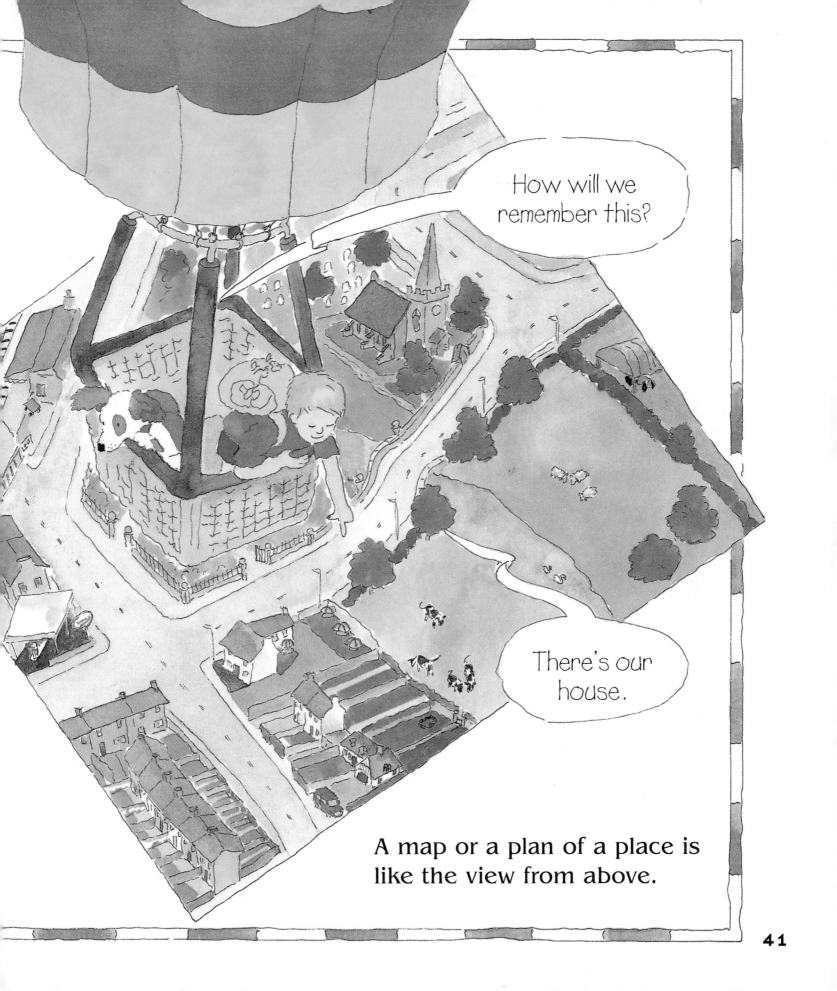

41

Drawing a plan

Harry and Ralph decide to make a plan of the garden. They can see its shape from above.

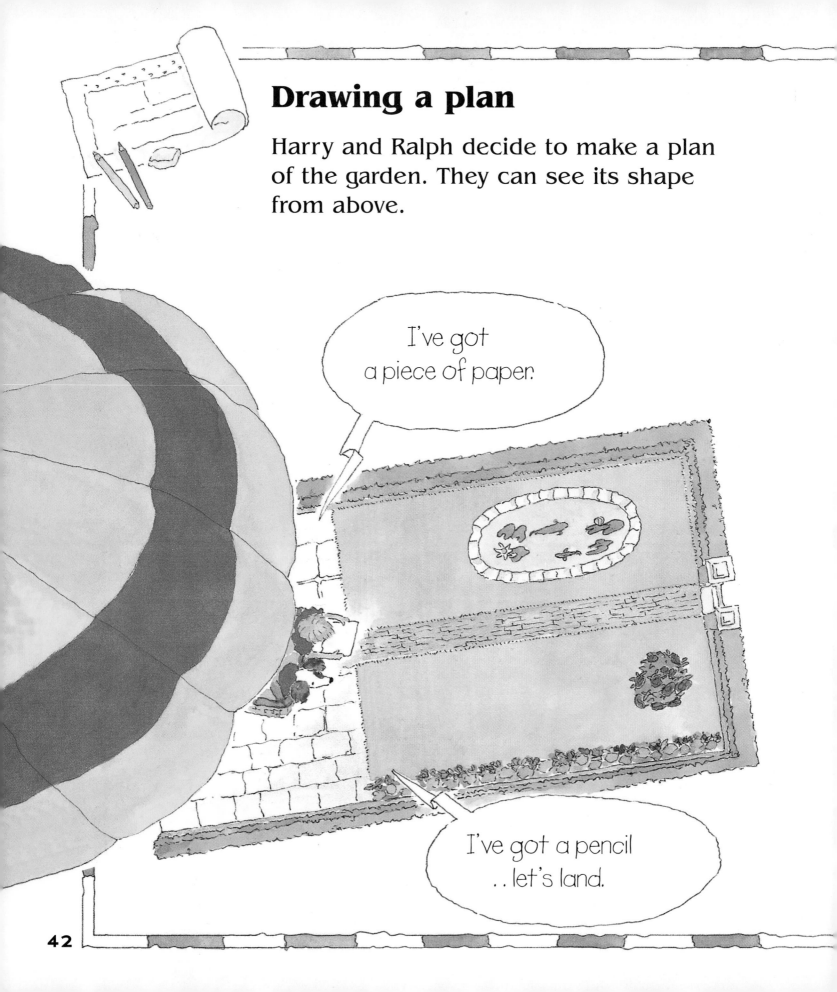

Harry walks from the front of the garden to the back. It is 30 steps long. Then he walks from one side to the other. It is 16 steps wide.

Harry draws his steps on the paper. Now he wants to put in the rose tree and the pond. How can he find out exactly where to put them?

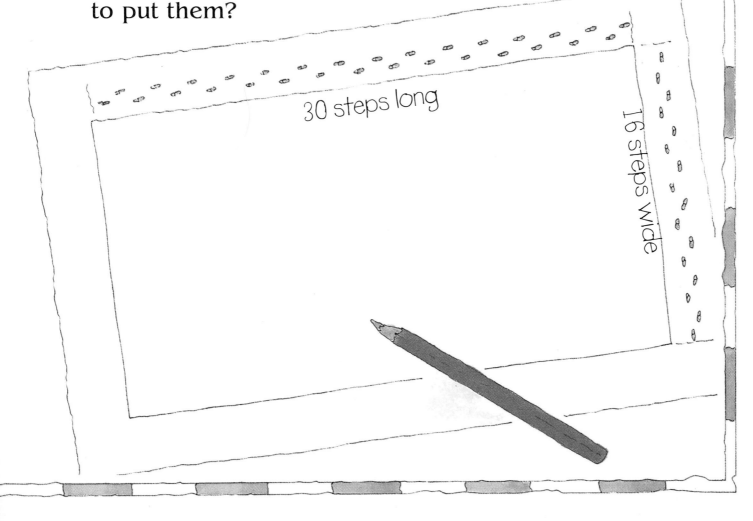

30 steps long

16 steps wide

Adding details

Harry counts his steps from one end of the garden to the rose tree—3 steps. Then he counts his steps from the side of the garden to the rose tree—4 steps.

Ralph marks the steps on his plan and draws in the rose tree. Then Harry finds out that the pond is 3 steps from the end and 1 step from the side. Ralph draws it in.

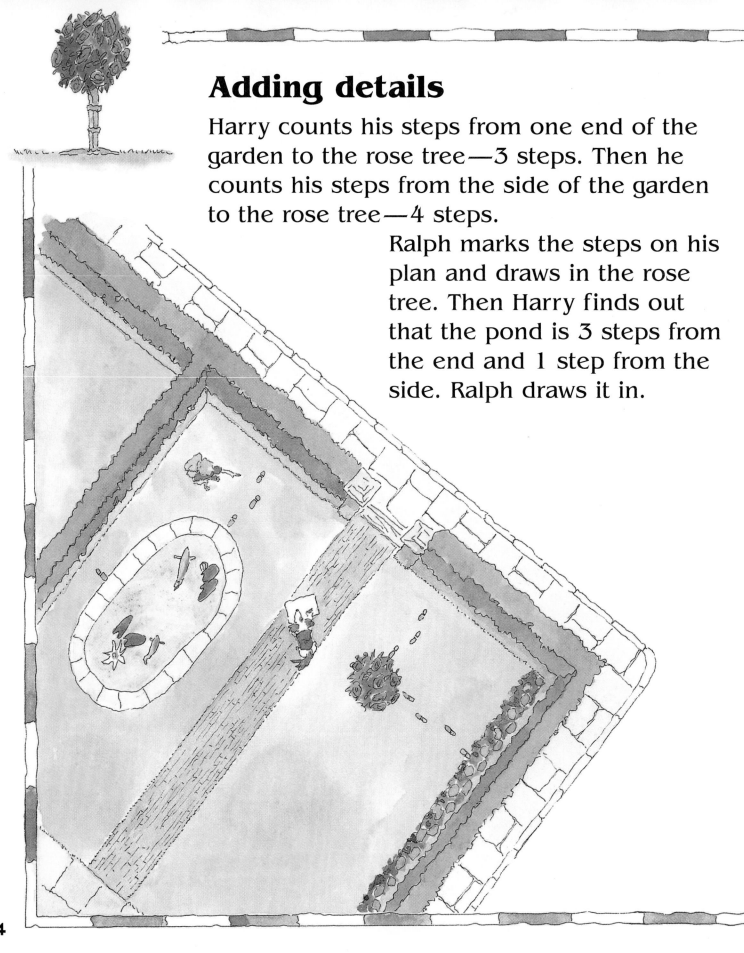

Ralph measures the garden with a tape measure. It is 60 feet (18 meters) long, which means that one of Harry's steps is 2 feet (0.6 meter) long. They draw a scale on their plan. Make a plan of your garden or your classroom.

2 feet

The route to school

Look at the picture opposite. It shows Harry's school at the top, the church in the middle, and Harry's house at the bottom. Below, Harry is making a map of his way, or route, to school.

He thinks hard about where he turns left and where he turns right. He draws in landmarks, which are special things like the bridge and the church that he sees on the way. He marks in his route.

Don't forget the big oak tree.

school

house

Now you do the same for a short trip that you know well.

The World's

a playground

Chicago, IL—When kids at Clissold Elementary need to check a map, they can just look out their school window. About 40 kids and grown-ups painted what may be one of the largest maps of the world right on the cement at their playground.

The kids first sketched out chalk lines, looked at lots of other maps as guides, and then carefully used a small paint machine. Only the outlines of the continents and waterways were finished with permanent paint. The rest was filled in by students with colored chalk.

Think About Reading

1. Who is Ralph?

2. Why do Harry and Ralph go up in a balloon?

3. Harry and Ralph look down from the balloon. What do they see that will not be on a map?

4. What do you think is the most important thing you learned about maps from this story?

5. How are Harry's maps different from the map in "The World's a Playground"?

Write a Postcard

Harry wants to show what he has learned. Help Harry write a postcard to a friend. Write about two things that Harry saw on his balloon ride. Draw a picture for the card, too.

Literature Circle

Think of a place you would like to go. Explain how a map or maps would help you.

Author
Kate Petty

Kate Petty knows that learning is fun, even when you're grown up. She learned a lot about geography while she was working on Around and About Maps and Journeys. Petty says she learns new things with every book she writes. She's learned a lot, because she has written more than 100 books!

More Books by
Kate Petty

- Feeling Left Out
- On a Plane
- Playing the Game

The day has just begun.
A white mist hangs over the park.
No one is here yet, and the park is very still.
Under a tree sits a single white park bench.

こうえんの　あさ。
きりが　しろい。みずも　しろい。
まだ　だれも　こない　こうえんは,
とても　しずか。
きの　したに,　しろい　ベンチが　ひとつ。

こうえんに　いちばんのりは，はやおきの　ひと。
たいそうを　する　ひと。いぬを　つれた　ひと。
しろい　ベンチも　めを　さます。
あ，いつもの　おじさんが，ちいさな　くるまで　やって

54

The early risers are the first to arrive.

Some do exercises. Others walk their dogs.

The white bench is just now waking up.

Look, here comes the park worker in his little motor cart.

"Good morning, my dear park bench,"
says the worker. "It's cleaning day for the
park," and he gives the bench a friendly
little pat.

Children pass by on their way to school.
Adults pass by on their way to work.
The town is becoming lively.

「やあ，おはよう，しろい　ベンチ。
きょうは，こうえんを
きれいに　する　ひだよ。」
ベンチを　ぽんと　たたいて，
おじさんは，しごとを　はじめる。

がっこうに　いく　ひとが　とおる。
かいしゃに　いく　ひとが　とおる。
まちが　にぎやかに　なって　くる。

こうえんに，おじいさんが　さんぽに　きた。
つえを　ついて　ゆっくり。
はなを　みたり，とりを　みたり，
いそがないで　ゆっくり。

「やれやれ，どっこいしょ。」
しろい　ベンチで　ひとやすみ。
「ちょうど　いい　ところに，
ちょうど　いい　ベンチが　あるね。」

Here comes an old man
taking his walk.
He moves very slowly,
leaning on his cane.
He stops to smell the flowers
and then to feed the birds.
He's not in any hurry.

"Now it's time for a rest,"
says the old man.
He sits on the white bench.
"The perfect bench in just
the right place," he thinks.

Along comes a mother and her baby.

"Let's sit in the sun," she says.

"The white bench is bathed in sunlight."

"Da, da," the baby babbles.

"Goo, goo," the old man replies.

What *can* they be talking about?

つぎに　きたのは，あかちゃんと　おかあさん。

「ひなたぼっこしましょ。

しろい　ベンチに　おひさまが　いっぱい。」

ばあ，ばあって　あかちゃん。

ほう，ほうって　おじいさん。

ふたりで　なんの　おはなしして　いるの？

Friends meet at the park.
The two mothers begin to chat.
They talk on and on.
Chitter-chatter, chitter-chatter, until it's time to eat.

All the while the white bench listens quietly.

こうえんで　であったら，

すぐに　おしゃべり　ぺちゃくちゃ。

いつに　なっても　おわらない。

おなかが　すくまで　ぺちゃくちゃ　ぺちゃくちゃ。

だまって　きいて　いる　しろい　ベンチ。

It's lunch time. The park worker eats under a large tree.
Here come the cats and the birds.
"Okay, my little friends. I'll give you some food," he says.
"But, oops, don't make the bench dirty."

こうえんの　きの　したで,

おじさんの　おひる。

ほら, あつまって　きた

のらねこたち, ことりたち。

「よしよし, いま　わけて　やるからな。

おっと, ベンチを　よごさないで　くれよ。」

ひるやすみの　こうえん。いろんな　ひとが　くる。

「ひるねには　やっぱり，この　ベンチが　いちばん　いいや。」

ふんわり　そよかぜが　いい　きもち。

ベンチも　いっしょに　うっとりする。

During the noon hour, lots of people come to the park to relax.
"This park bench is my favorite spot for a nap," says a man.
A gentle breeze is blowing, and the park bench begins
to feel drowsy, too.

A young man waits for his friend who is late.
"Let's meet in the park, at the white bench,"
they had agreed. "But now, where can she be?"

("Wait, who left a book on the bench?"
the park worker wonders.)

「こうえんで　あおうね。

いつもの　しろい　ベンチでね。」って

やくそくしたのに, なかなか　こない　ともだち。

やくそく　わすれて　いないかなあ。

(おや, ベンチの　うえに　だれかの　わすれもの。)

Here comes a group of children running to the park.
This is the liveliest time of day.
"What are we going to play today?" asks one child.
"Let's talk it over."

こどもたちが　おおぜい　やって　きた。

こうえんが　いちばん　にぎやかに　なる　じかん。

「きょうは，なに　して　あそぶ?」

「そうだんしよう。しろい　ベンチに

みんな　あつまれー！」

71

しろい　ベンチは，おうちに　なる。おしろに　なる。

しまに　なる。ふねに　なる。でんしゃに　なる。

えきに　なる。　それから　ベンチにも　なる。

All of a sudden the white bench becomes a house.

Now it's a castle, then an island, now a boat.

Now a train. Then a station.

And then, it's even a park bench again!

Plip plop, plip plop . . .
"Uh-oh, here it comes," says the worker to himself.

Suddenly, it begins to rain. Everyone runs for shelter.
Everyone except, of course, the white bench.

ぽつん，ぽつん，ぱららん……。
「おっ，ふって　きたかな。」

あめ，あめ，にわかあめ。
はしって，はしって，あまやどり。
きが　ぬれる。しばふが　ぬれる。
しろい　ベンチも　あめの　なか。

The rain has stopped.
Now the sky is bright.
The wet flowers and grass glisten.
"You're soaking wet," says the park worker
to the bench, as he gently wipes it dry.
"You're a fine bench in spite of your age," he says.
"I know you'll last for a long, long time."

あめが　やんだ。　まぶしい　そら。

はなにも，　くさにも，

ひかる　しずくが　いっぱい。

「おやおや，　びしょぬれだ。」

おじさんが　ベンチを　ふいて　くれたよ。

「ずいぶん　ふるく　なったけど，

いい　ベンチだからなあ。

まだまだ　がんばって　くれよ。」

こうえんの　ゆうぐれ。　ちょっぴり　かぜが　つめたく　なる。

「また　あしたね。」って　てを　ふって,

こどもたちが　かえって　いく。

しろい　ベンチも　ゆうぐれの　いろ。

Now the day is ending.

The air becomes chilly.

Children wave to each other as they leave for home.

The white park bench is perfectly still in the twilight.

When the lights go on in the town,
the worker's day is done.
"Good night, my dear white bench,"
he says. "You must be very tired.
I'll see you tomorrow."
He turns on the lights of his little
motor cart and drives home.

まちに　あかりが　ともる　ころ，
おじさんの　しごとも　おしまいだ。
「さよなら，しろい　ベンチ。
きょうも　いちにち　おつかれさま。
じゃ，また　くるよ。」
ちいさな　くるまに　ライトを　つけて，
おじさんが　かえって　いく。

The park is covered with darkness.
Stars twinkle in the sky.
No one is here now, and the park is very still.
Under a tree sits a single white park bench.

Good night.

こうえんの　よる。

そらに　ほしが　きらり　きらり。

もう　だれも　いない　こうえんは,

とても　しずか。

きの　したに,　しろい　ベンチが　ひとつ。

おやすみなさい。

 Read Together!

Steve Yamashiro

Mayor

**Steve Yamashiro is the mayor of Hilo, Hawaii.
A mayor makes sure everybody is safe and can enjoy
the town they live in.**

Mayor Yamashiro does his paperwork and has meetings in his office.

As mayor, Steve Yamashiro spends time with people who live in his town.

"The best thing about being mayor is I work with many people," says Steve Yamashiro. "We make changes for everyone who lives here."

Think About Reading

1. Who is the first person to stop at the white bench in the morning?

2. Why do the mother and her baby sit on the bench with the old man?

3. How does the white bench become a castle?

4. Why do you think the park worker talks to the white bench?

5. How is the park worker like Mayor Steve Yamashiro?

Write an Award

The park worker takes very good care of the white bench. He should get an award. Draw an award for the worker. Write a sentence about the man's good work. You may wish to name the award and tell why it is important.

Literature Circle

How does the park in the story change throughout the day? What time of day would you most like to visit the park? Why?

Illustrator
Mamoru Suzuki

Mamoru Suzuki is a well-known artist in Japan. He has worked with writer Fumiko Takeshita on several children's books. Suzuki likes watching the way light changes during the day. In The Park Bench, he used light and shadow to show different times of day in the park.

More Books Illustrated by
Mamoru Suzuki

- Will Chip Stay Home?
- Chip Goes to the Seaside
- Wayside Friends

LITTLE BEAR

by

ELSE HOLMELUND MINARIK

pictures by MAURICE SENDAK

An I CAN READ Book®

Birthday Soup

"Mother Bear,

Mother Bear,

Where are you?" calls Little Bear.

"Oh, dear, Mother Bear is not here,

and today is my birthday.

"I think my friends will come,

but I do not see a birthday cake.

My goodness—no birthday cake.

What can I do?

"The pot is by the fire.

The water in the pot is hot.

If I put something in the water,

I can make Birthday Soup.

All my friends like soup.

"Let me see what we have.

We have carrots and potatoes,

peas and tomatoes;

I can make soup with

carrots, potatoes, peas and tomatoes."

So Little Bear begins to make soup

in the big black pot.

First, Hen comes in.

"Happy Birthday, Little Bear," she says.

"Thank you, Hen," says Little Bear.

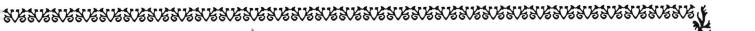

Hen says, "My! Something smells good here.

Is it in the big black pot?"

"Yes," says Little Bear,

"I am making Birthday Soup.

Will you stay and have some?"

"Oh, yes, thank you," says Hen.

And she sits down to wait.

Next, Duck comes in.

"Happy Birthday, Little Bear," says Duck.

"My, something smells good.

Is it in the big black pot?"

"Thank you, Duck," says Little Bear.

"Yes, I am making Birthday Soup.

Will you stay and have some with us?"

"Thank you, yes, thank you," says Duck.

And she sits down to wait.

Next, Cat comes in.

"Happy Birthday, Little Bear," he says.

"Thank you, Cat," says Little Bear.

"I hope you like Birthday Soup.

I am making Birthday Soup."

Cat says, "Can you really cook?

If you can really make it,

I will eat it."

"Good," says Little Bear.

"The Birthday Soup is hot,

so we must eat it now.

We cannot wait for Mother Bear.

I do not know where she is."

"Now, here is some soup for you, Hen,"

says Little Bear.

"And here is some soup for you, Duck,

"and here is some soup for you, Cat,

and here is some soup for me.

Now we can all have some Birthday Soup."

Cat sees Mother Bear at the door,

and says, "Wait, Little Bear.

Do not eat yet.

Shut your eyes, and say one, two, three."

Little Bear shuts his eyes

and says, "One, two, three."

Mother Bear comes in with a big cake.

"Now, look," says Cat.

"Oh, Mother Bear," says Little Bear,

"what a big beautiful Birthday Cake!

Birthday Soup is good to eat,

but not as good as Birthday Cake.

I am so happy you did not forget."

"Yes, Happy Birthday, Little Bear!"
says Mother Bear.

"This Birthday Cake is a surprise for you.

I never did forget your birthday,

and I never will."

two friends

lydia and shirley have
two pierced ears and
two bare ones
five pigtails
two pairs of sneakers
two berets
two smiles
one necklace
one bracelet
lots of stripes and
one good friendship

Nikki Giovanni

THINK ABOUT READING

1. What does Little Bear use to make Birthday Soup?

2. Why does Little Bear make Birthday Soup?

3. How do you think Little Bear feels about not having a birthday cake?

4. Look at the last picture. How do you think Little Bear feels?

5. How are the girls in "two friends" like Little Bear and his friends?

WRITE A STORY BEGINNING

What else does Little Bear do with his friends? What will he do after his birthday party? There are many other stories about Little Bear. You can make up your own. Write the beginning of your story on another piece of paper. Draw a picture to show how your story ends.

LITERATURE CIRCLE

How can you tell that the animals in Birthday Soup are good friends? How can you tell that the girls in "two friends" like each other? What do you think friends can do for each other?

ILLUSTRATOR
MAURICE SENDAK

Photograph © 1988 by Chris Callis

Maurice Sendak believes a lively imagination is important for an artist. He has illustrated over ninety books and has won three important awards (the Caldecott Medal, the Hans Christian Andersen Award, and the Laura Ingalls Wilder Medal). At an early age Maurice Sendak decided to spend his life illustrating and making books—and he has been doing so ever since.

MORE BOOKS by
MAURICE SENDAK

- Where the Wild Things Are
- Alligators All Around
- In the Night Kitchen
- Pierre
- Chicken Soup with Rice

Stone Soup

a French folk tale retold
by Adrienne Betz

illustrated by John O'Brien

SCHOLASTIC

Once upon a time, a poor woman and her son were very far from home. Their names were Marie and Henri, and they had traveled a long, long way. They had no food. They were so hungry!

At last they came to a town. The travelers went from house to house and asked, "Friend, do you have a bit of food to spare?"

"No!" said the woman at the first house.

"No!" said the man at the second house.

"No!" said the little girl who peeked out from behind the door at the third house.

The hungry travelers asked the baker,
the tailor, and the shoemaker.

The baker said, "No!"

The tailor said, "No!"

The shoemaker said, "No!"

They even asked at the mayor's house,
and even the mayor said, "No, I have
nothing to share!"

"Mr. Mayor," said Henri. "Your town must be very poor! No one has as much as a crust of bread to share."

"But we will help you," said Marie. "We know a way to feed your whole town. All we need is a big pot. Do you have one?"

The mayor called to his children, "Bring out our big pot!"

He opened his door wide. The children came out carrying the BIGGEST pot the travelers had ever seen.

"Thank you, my friends!" said Marie.

MAYOR

The travelers carried the pot to the center of town. Henri filled the pot with water. Marie built a fire around the pot. Everyone in town came out to watch them.

"Welcome, friends," said Marie. "Please, join us! My dear son and I are going to make a very special soup for you. It's called stone soup."

Then, as everyone watched, Marie bent down, picked up a stone, and dropped it right into the pot.

The baker said, "Impossible!"

The tailor said, "Impossible!"

The shoemaker said, "Impossible!"

"No one can make soup from a stone!"
said the mayor.

"Watch and learn, my friends," said Marie with a smile.

Then she took a big spoon out of her traveling bag. She used the spoon to stir the pot.

"Ah," said Henri. "There's nothing as good as stone soup! Of course, it would be even BETTER if we had a carrot. But where would we ever find one?"

"I think I know where to find a carrot!" said one woman.

"Thank you, my friend," Marie said. "This would be the perfect time to add carrots to the soup."

The woman raced home and came back
with a bunch of carrots.

Marie quickly sliced the carrots and stirred
them into the soup.

"Ah," said Henri. "There's nothing as good as stone soup! Of course, it would be even BETTER if we had a potato. But where would we ever find one?"

"I think I know where to find a potato!" said a man.

"Thank you, my friend," Marie said. "This would be the perfect time to add potatoes to the soup."

The man raced home and came back with a sack of potatoes.

Marie quickly sliced the potatoes and stirred them into the soup.

"Ah," said Henri, "there's nothing as good as stone soup! Of course, it would be even BETTER if we had a few beans. But where would we ever find some?"

"I'll bring some beans," said a little girl.

"I don't have any beans," said a little boy. "But I do have some cabbage!"

Now everyone in town thought of something that he or she could bring.

Marie quickly sliced and stirred all the good things into the soup. The soup was now so thick that it was hard to stir it.

"We can help," said the baker, the tailor, and the shoemaker. They all took turns stirring the pot.

At last the soup was ready!

Again everyone raced home. This time they came back with bowls and spoons. Marie used her big spoon to fill each bowl.

The mayor was the very first to try the soup. "Mmmmmm," said the mayor. "It's amazing! Soup from a stone!"

"Mmmmmmm," said the townspeople. "It's amazing AND delicious!"

They all ate and ate until they could not eat
any more. Then everyone sang songs and laughed
together until the stars came out.

The mayor made a speech. "We all thank you!" he said to Marie and Henri. "Please stay in our town as long as you like!"

That night, the travelers went home with the
mayor and his family. They were given the finest
beds in the house.

"Ah," said Henri to his mother as she tucked him in. "There's nothing as good as stone soup, ESPECIALLY when you have friends to share it with you!"

Think About Reading

Think about <u>Stone Soup</u>. Finish each sentence in the story map. Do your work on another piece of paper.

Beginning

1. _____ and _____ come to a town.

2. They are _____, but _____ _____ will give them food.

Middle

3. They start cooking a pot of _____ _____.

4. People from the town add _____, _____, _____, _____, and other things to the soup.

End

5. _____ eats the stone soup.

Write a Recipe

What if you and your friends were making stone soup? What would you add to the soup? Write your own recipe for stone soup on another piece of paper. Write this information:

- The name of the recipe.
- What we will add to it.
- How to cook it.

STONE SOUP
1 stone
lots of water
cook together

Literature Circle

How do Marie and Henri get help from the people of the town? What else could Marie and Henri do to get help? How do you think that would turn out?

Illustrator
John O'Brien

Some artists draw pictures for children. Other artists draw pictures for grown-ups. John O'Brien does both! He likes drawing pictures for children's books. He draws special coloring books for children, too. He also likes drawing pictures for magazines with news, facts, and stories.

More Books Illustrated by
John O'Brien

- The Reptile Ball
- Six Sleepy Sheep
- Daffy Down Dillies: Silly Limericks

GLOS

You will find all your vocabulary words in ABC order in the Glossary. This page shows you how to use it.

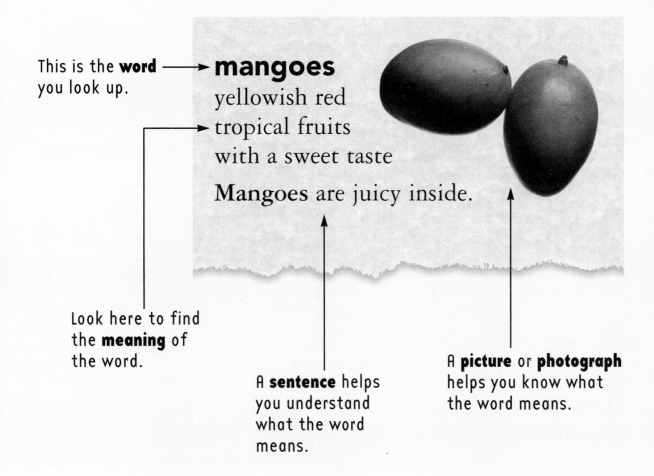

This is the **word** you look up. →

mangoes

yellowish red tropical fruits with a sweet taste

Mangoes are juicy inside.

Look here to find the **meaning** of the word.

A **sentence** helps you understand what the word means.

A **picture** or **photograph** helps you know what the word means.

adults

people who are grown-up

Most **adults** can drive cars.

baby

a very young child

The **baby** sleeps in a crib.

back

the opposite end of front

My desk is at the **back** of the classroom.

beans

seeds or pods that grow on plants

Mom makes chili with **beans** and meat.

beans

bear

a large, heavy, wild animal with thick fur

The brown **bear** lives in the forest.

bottom

the lowest point or part of something

Kim wrote her name at the **bottom** of the page.

bread

a baked food made from flour, water, and other things

I used two pieces of **bread** to make a sandwich.

cake

a sweet, baked food made with flour, butter, eggs, and sugar

Put a candle on the **cake**.

child

a young boy or girl

A **child** grows up to become an adult.

children

young boys or girls

Most **children** like school.

cook

to make and heat food

Grandma will **cook** dinner for us.

down

from a higher to a lower place

The book fell **down** from the shelf.

eat

to take in food through your mouth

I **eat** breakfast in the morning.

family

a group of people who are related to each other

Tia's **family** includes her mother, father, brother, and grandfather.

food

the things people and animals eat to stay alive and grow

Pizza is Mandy's favorite **food**.

friends

people who know and like each other

Juan's **friends** came to his birthday party.

front

the part of something that comes first or faces forward

Our doorbell is at the **front** of our house.

hungry

wanting food

Jamal ate lunch early because he was **hungry**.

mangoes

yellowish red tropical fruits with a sweet taste

Mangoes are juicy inside.

mangoes

market

a place where people buy and sell food or other things

Mario bought milk at the **market**.

middle

the place halfway between two places or things

My nose is in the **middle** of my face, between my forehead and chin.

people

human beings

Men, women, and children are **people**.

poor

having little or no money

Poor is the opposite of rich.

smells

gives off a scent or an odor

A rose **smells** nice.

soup

a liquid food made with vegetables, meat, or fish

Please pour some **soup** in my bowl.

top

the highest point or part of something

Put the candles on the **top** of the cake.

village

a very small place where people live and work

A **village** is smaller than a town.

water

the colorless liquid that falls as rain and fills oceans, rivers and lakes

Drink some **water** if you're thirsty.

women

adult female people

Mothers and aunts are **women**.

worker

someone who does a job

A zoo **worker** feeds and takes care of the animals.

Acknowledgments

Grateful acknowledgment is made to the following sources for permission to reprint from previously published material. The publisher has made diligent efforts to trace the ownership of all copyrighted material in this volume and believes that all necessary permissions have been secured. If any errors or omissions have inadvertently been made, proper corrections will gladly be made in future editions.

"It Takes A Village" from IT TAKES A VILLAGE by Jane Cowen-Fletcher. Copyright © 1994 by Jane Cowen-Fletcher. Used by permission of Scholastic Inc.

"Kiosco de cerezas/Cherry Stand" from GATHERING THE SUN by Alma Flor Ada. Text copyright © 1997 by Alma Flor Ada. English translations copyright © 1997 by Rosa Zubizarreta. Illustrations copyright © 1997 by Simon Silva. Reprinted by permission of Lothrop, Lee & Shepard Books, a division of William Morrow & Company, Inc.

"Maps and Journeys" from AROUND AND ABOUT MAPS AND JOURNEYS by Kate Petty and Jakki Wood. Copyright © 1993 by Aladdin Books, Ltd. Designed and produced by Aladdin Books Ltd., London. Published by Barron's Educational Series, Inc. Hauppauge, NY. Reprinted by permission.

"The World's a Playground" from KID CITY® MAGAZINE, June 1993. Copyright © 1993 Children's Television Workshop (New York, NY). All rights reserved.

"The Park Bench" from THE PARK BENCH by Fumiko Takeshita, illustrated by Mamoru Suziki, translated by Ruth A. Kanagy. Copyright © Fumiko Takeshita/Mamoru Suzuki. American text copyright © 1988 by Kane/Miller Book Publishers. Reprinted by permission of Kane/Miller Book Publishers.

"Little Bear: 'Birthday Soup'" from LITTLE BEAR by Else Holmelund Minarik, illustrations by Maurice Sendak. Text copyright © 1957 by Else Holmelund Minarik. Illustrations copyright © 1957 by Maurice Sendak. Reprinted by permission of HarperCollins Children's Books, a division of HarperCollins Publishers.

"Two Friends" from SPIN A SOFT BLACK SONG by Nikki Giovanni. Copyright © 1985 by Nikki Giovanni. Reprinted by permission of Farrar, Straus & Giroux, Inc.

"Stone Soup" from STONE SOUP by Adrienne Betz, illustrated by John O'Brien. Copyright © 1996 by Scholastic Inc. Reprinted by permission of Scholastic Inc.

Photography and Illustration Credits

Photos: pp. 6tl, 7br, 84ml, 84bl, 84c, Joe Carini for Scholastic Inc.; p. 6br, © David Cornwell/Pacific Stock; p. 6tr, © Rita Ariyoshi/Pacific Stock; p. 6br, © Kyle Rothenborg/ Pacific Stock; p. 6tl, © Greg Vaughn/ Pacific Stock; p. 7bl, © Greg Vaughn/ Pacific Stock; p. 37, Pria Nair for Scholastic Inc.

Cover: John O'Brien for Scholastic Inc.

Illustrations: pp.2–3,130–131:John O'Brien for Scholastic Inc. p.4: Leo Manahan for Scholastic Inc. pp 6–7: Jackie Snider for Scholastic Inc. pp.104–105:Susan Keeter for Scholastic Inc.

Illustrated Author Photos: p.37: Gabe DiFiore for Scholastic Inc. pp. 86,107,131: David Franck for Scholastic Inc.